GLADIATOR

First published 2007 by
A & C Black Publishers Ltd
38 Soho Square, London, W1D 3HB

www.acblack.com

Text copyright © 2007 Helen Greathead
Illustrations copyright © 2007 Bob Dewar

The rights of Helen Greathead and Bob Dewar to
be identified as the author and illustrator of this work
have been asserted by them in accordance with the
Copyrights, Designs and Patents Act 1988.

ISBN 978-0-7136-7774-4 (hbk)
ISBN 978-0-7136-7771-3 (pbk)

A CIP catalogue for this book is available
from the British Library.

This book is produced using paper that is made from
wood grown in managed, sustainable forests. It is natural,
renewable and recyclable. The logging and manufacturing
processes conform to the environmental regulations
of the country of origin.

Printed and bound by MPG Books Ltd, Bodmin, Cornwall.

TOUGH JOBS
GLADIATOR

Helen Greathead
Illustrated by Bob Dewar

A & C Black • London

WELCOME TO THE ROMAN EMPIRE

Imagine a time when:

• People didn't have electricity – but they did have running water.

• People didn't build skyscrapers – but they did build some huge structures that are still standing today.

• People didn't go to football matches in gigantic stadiums – but they did go to watch fights in huge arenas. These fights were man against man ... to the death.

The Roman Empire began over 2000 years ago, when the Romans started to attack and take over other lands. The Empire lasted over 500 years. It stretched from Egypt all the way to Wales.

Rome was the capital city of the Empire, the biggest city on earth. Over a million people lived there – Roman citizens and slaves. Some of these slaves, and a few Roman citizens, risked a horrible death for the chance to get rich and famous – they were the ones called gladiators.

STAR-STRUCK!

Let's pretend you are a Roman citizen. You, your family and over 30 slaves live in a big, smart house slap bang in the centre of Rome.

Your dad works in the Senate, doing important government stuff, and you hardly ever see him. But today is a special day. It's a festival. There are games at the Colosseum, and your dad is taking you out!

Is he taking you to see the gladiators? Of course not! Your dad doesn't approve of the games. He thinks they set a bad example. And, anyway, he doesn't like you mixing with poor people.

"Come on," your dad says. "Let's go to the public baths."

Oh dear, you know what this means – your dad wants to talk to you about something serious.

But at the baths, your dad keeps bumping into people from the Senate. You don't speak to each other at all.

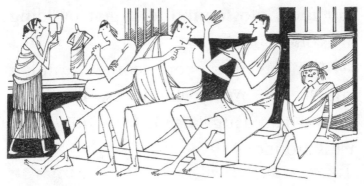

"I have been thinking about your future," your dad says, at last, as you head for home.

"Oh?" you answer.

"What are you going to be?" Your dad looks thoughtful. "Have you the brains to get into the Senate, like me? Or would you make a better soldier?"

"I hadn't really thought—" you start.

"From now on I've decided to teach you myself," your dad interrupts. "Then I can find out what you're really made of."

Suddenly, you hear a huge cheer, followed by chants of "Felix! Felix! Felix!" You notice you are walking past the Colosseum, the largest building in Rome!

Moments later, people come streaming out of the many entrances. They are talking and laughing and waving their arms around.

Your dad spots yet another of his friends and rushes to greet him. Marcus is one of the organisers of the games and he is very, very rich. He's with his son, Max, and you cannot believe what happens next.

"What did you think of the games?" Marcus asks your dad.

"Um…" your dad hesitates.

"Fantastic, weren't they?" Marcus says, answering his own question.

"But the next games will be even better," says Max. "'Cos Dad's going to be the editor."

"Max is the biggest fan of all," says Marcus. "He knows everything there is to know about the games. In fact, I've pulled a few strings so he can go and say hello to Felix now."

"Why don't you come, too?" Max asks eagerly. You look at your dad, expecting him to say no, but he lets you go happily.

Max is a bit older than you and already twice as big. You follow him around the Colosseum, and find yourself in front of the main gladiator school. He pushes to the front of the crowd, just in time to see the security guard lock the gates.

"There's Felix!" he shouts.

If Max is big, Felix is enormous. He looks amazing. He starts strolling up and down, his armour sparkling, swishing his purple cape. He smiles and waves.

You are completely and utterly star-struck. If only you could see him in action … but how?

Suddenly, Felix sees Max, and strides over to join him. "Sorry I missed you, Max" he says. "Why don't you join my lesson at sunrise tomorrow?"

"Can my friend come, too?" Max asks.

Felix looks at you and smiles. "You're welcome, as long as your father approves," he says.

Wow, the most famous person in Rome just spoke to you! Felix swings round before you manage to reply. But somehow, whatever your dad says, you know you'll be there in the morning.

WHO'D BE A GLADIATOR?

Three types of people can become gladiators:

Slaves – If the owner of the gladiator school wants some new trainees, he sends someone off to the slave market. They will look for a slave who is strong and fit. Prisoners of war are best – if the slave can fight already, he will be easy to train.

Criminals – Some criminals are sentenced to fight in the arena. It's better than being sentenced to death – at least they get a chance to fight back. But only the strongest, fittest criminals are trained. The rest are given armour and weapons, then thrown straight into the arena. Hardly any come out alive.

Roman Citizens – A citizen who can't pay his taxes, or has lost his family's money, might choose to become a gladiator. The gladiator school pays him to train there. The money he gets will pay off some debts and – with a lot of luck and training – he could get rich again.

Roman citizens look down on gladiators – unless they are very, very good indeed!

GLADIATOR SCHOOL

Your dad doesn't want you to visit the gladiator school again, but once you tell him Max is going, he's suddenly a pushover!

Max is already in the queue when you arrive. He's standing in front of a group of girls. "Are they here for lessons, too?" you joke.

"I don't think so," says Max. "I have seen women fight, though. They're not a patch on the men!"

The gates swing open and you enter a very large courtyard, with an arena inside.

Felix enters, with an older man. The girls rush past you, screaming. They gather round Felix, sighing and tugging at his tunic. So that's why they're here. They fancy Felix!

Up close, Felix towers above you. His arms are as thick as your head and his legs are like tree trunks. "Morning, everyone," he says.

The old bloke who arrived with Felix starts to talk: "Welcome to the Ludus Magnus, where over 500 gladiators live and train…"

"Who's he?" you ask Max.

"He's in charge of the gladiators," says Max. "Everyone calls him Papa."

You wonder why. He doesn't look very nice.

"…This is our practice arena," Papa continues, "which seats a small audience of 3,000 people."

"If that's small, what's the main arena like?" you whisper.

Max stretches his arms as far as they'll go. "Huge!" he says.

The girls sit at the side, while you boys get down to business. An armourer appears from underneath the arena and hands you each a wooden sword and wicker shield.

"Attack the stake with the sword," says Felix, waving towards some tall wooden posts. "I want to see what you can do."

You don't know where to start, but you fly at the post, hitting it with your sword.

Felix wanders around watching you all. Then he puts you and Max together for a trial fight.

"We might train you as a Secutor gladiator," he tells Max. "You'd wear a heavy helmet, which makes seeing and running around quite difficult, but you'd be well protected." He turns to you. "You're smaller and lighter, so we could train you as a Retiarius gladiator. You wouldn't wear much armour, so you'd need to move quickly!"

He leaves you to your fight. But Max knocks you to the ground before you have a chance to run.

Felix marches straight back. He looks cross and you're sure he's going to ask you to leave. But he turns to Max. "That move might save your skin," he says, "but the crowd would be furious. They want fancy footwork and clever moves – you have to entertain them!"

Felix teaches you how to hold the sword and shield properly. By the end of the morning you are getting the hang of it – and you finally knock Max down. Hurray!

You've also made an important decision. When you grow up, you won't be a soldier or a senator, you are going to be … a gladiator!

GLADIATOR WHO'S WHO

There are many different types of gladiator. Here are some of the most popular:

Secutor means "one who chases", he usually fights **Retiarius**, who gets his name from the net he carries.

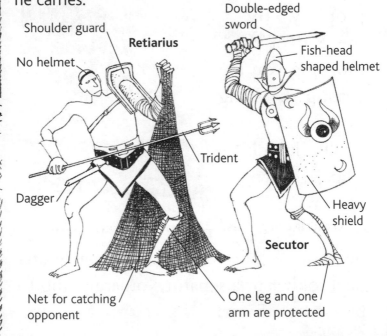

Double-edged sword

Fish-head shaped helmet

Shoulder guard

Retiarius

No helmet

Trident

Dagger

Heavy shield

Secutor

Net for catching opponent

One leg and one arm are protected

The **Thracian** uses the equipment of Rome's old enemies, the Thracian warriors. He usually fights **Murmillo**, who is named after a type of fish!

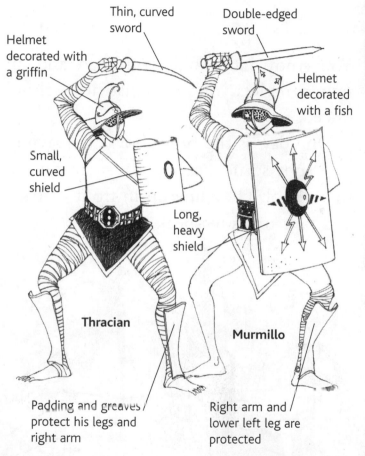

Helmet decorated with a griffin

Thin, curved sword

Double-edged sword

Helmet decorated with a fish

Small, curved shield

Long, heavy shield

Thracian

Murmillo

Padding and greaves protect his legs and right arm

Right arm and lower left leg are protected

All gladiators wear a type of loincloth, held up with a large belt. It's a fancy version of ancient Roman underwear!

NEW RECRUITS

You study hard with your dad and, in return, he lets you go to gladiator school once a week.

One day, as the other boys are leaving, you spot some new recruits arriving at the school. They line up in front of Papa and take turns to speak.

"What's happening?" you ask.

"Let's hide behind this pillar and see," says Max.

Two of the men have chains around their ankles.

The first is a curly haired young man, called Fabius.

The second is called Julius. He isn't in chains and he's wearing smart, Roman clothes.

The third is young, strong, handsome and serious. You listen carefully as he speaks to Papa.

"My name is Sura," he says, proudly. "For the next five years, I solemnly swear to obey you in everything, to suffer burning, imprisonment, flogging and even death by the sword."

"What?" you whisper to Max. "That's terrible. What do they get in return?"

"You now belong to my gladiator family," Papa says. "You will train daily. I shall feed you and keep you in top, fighting condition! And at the next games, in three months' time, you will fight – for your lives."

"That's not fair," whispers Max. "Most gladiators get six months to train!"

The three men are taken straight to the practice posts, unchained and given wooden swords and wicker shields. Two older men stand around, watching every move they make.

"The doctors will want to see what they can do," Max whispers.

"Doctors," you say, confused, "but they're not ill."

"I don't mean medical doctors," laughs Max. "They're instructors – experienced gladiators – the ones who've survived!"

Fabius skips about, jabbing at the post – and missing! Julius has a bit more skill, but he's very nervous.

But you can't take your eyes off Sura. He dances round his post, attacking every part of a pretend body. He twists, turns, slashes, stabs.

The doctors soon gather around him. Felix joins them and they talk seriously. Then Felix leaves with one of the armourers.

Ten minutes later, the armourer returns, loaded up with armour. Behind him walks a real, live Murmillo gladiator! Wow! You've never seen one so close before. A fantastic helmet covers his face. He carries an enormous sword and shield. And he is coming straight for you!

You shouldn't really be here, you both should have left ages ago. The gladiator stops right next to you and Max. Help! What will he do to you?

He lifts his visor. Phew – it's only Felix! He won't tell you off, as long as you're with Max. Everyone wants to keep in with Max's dad.

"You boys still here?" Felix smiles. "This fight will be worth watching. Sura is as good as a trained soldier. Better, in fact! We're going to try him out with some serious weapons. Hold this!" He hands you a sword.

You can barely lift it.

"We're fighting with iron practice swords." Felix explains. "We use them to build up a gladiator's strength. They're twice as heavy as a normal sword. In a real fight, a lighter weapon will speed Sura's moves and give him confidence."

You hear Papa talking to Sura: "So your grandfather was a Thracian?" he sneers. "Let's see if he taught you to fight like one."

Sura is dressed in full armour and padding, clutching the curved iron sword and shield. He gives Felix a cold stare, then the two creep round in a circle. Felix lifts his sword. Sura raises his shield and quicksteps round him. They clash. They circle each other. Sura struggles with the weight of his sword, but he still moves quickly. Felix's armour is heavier than Sura's, but he is used to it and can match Sura's speedy moves.

Suddenly, Felix has Sura on the floor … the fight is over.

TOUGH JOBS AT GLADIATOR SCHOOL

Procurator – is the top job. He only takes orders from the Emperor, and he looks after the staff, money and paperwork.

Lanista – is next in line. He is in charge of the "family" of gladiators. He's the one who finds new slaves for training. He organises the games – with the help of a rich "editor" from outside the school, who puts up the money for the games ... and gets all the glory.

There are plenty of jobs for retired or wounded gladiators:

Cooks – cooking is easy. The gladiators eat the same old barley and bean mush every day.

Instructors – are known as "doctors". Some teach a particular type of gladiator. Others teach the use of a particular type of weapon.

Security guards – watch over the weapons in a separate building – well away from any unhappy gladiators.

Then there are:

Armourers – who make the school's weapons and keep them all in tip-top condition.

Medical doctors – the school has real doctors and masseurs, too. The lanista wants to keep his gladiators fit and healthy. Not because he cares about them, but because good gladiators are worth a lot of money!

Scribes and **accountants** help with the day-to-day running of the school.

HOW TO DIE

Even Papa was impressed with Sura's first fight. Sura stayed on his feet for five whole minutes. That's excellent for a beginner! For the last two months he's been working hard with the other trainees. The games are now only four weeks away!

You try to go to the school as often as you can. Nobody seems to mind when you turn up, or how long you stay, as long as you're with Max.

Today you've been learning some fancy footwork. Now training has finished, you're watching Fabius. He's trying to juggle with swords!

"I'm going to use a few tricks to win over the audience," he says. Suddenly, he drops one of the swords – and it lands on Sura's foot! Sura screws up his face for a second, then straightens it again. He's obviously in pain.

Papa is disgusted. "Take this wimp to the medic," he orders.

You and Max do as you're told. You don't want to get on the wrong side of Papa.

"How did you end up here?" you ask Sura as you head off, each holding an arm to support him.

"I was a slave," says Sura. "I tried to run away, but they caught me. They sent me here as punishment."

"Is that why Papa keeps his trainees in chains?" asks Max.

"And the weapons in a separate building?" you add.

Sura nods. "An escaped gladiator could cause a load of trouble."

You pass a corridor lined with small rooms. They don't have windows and they're empty, except for a couple of bales of straw.

"I didn't know they kept animals," you say.

"They don't," laughs Sura. "This is where I sleep – in a room with Fabius."

On the next floor, through a doorway, you look into a well-furnished apartment. There's a woman in there with a baby!

"That's where Felix lives, with his wife and kids," says Sura.

"I think you should get star treatment, too," you say.

"Oh, don't worry," Sura smiles, "I intend to."

At the end of a corridor, you hear a long, deep groan. "Sounds like the medical rooms are this way!" says Max. "Look, there are loads of them!"

In one room, the groaning man is being pushed about by a huge masseur. In the next, you spot all kinds of horrible-looking tools and pull a face.

"It's all right," says Sura, "you don't have to stay."

"Good," says Max, running up the stairs to the top floor. "I need to pee." He soon hops back down again. "Nothing but offices up there. Rows of men scribbling away."

Back on the ground floor, you race past the kitchen and dining hall and find yourselves on the far side of the arena.

"Urgh! What's that smell?" you ask.

"The latrines!" Max answers, following his nose down the steps.

Felix, Fabius and Julius are in there already. They're chatting about the coming games.

"You thought of a name yet?" asks Felix, washing the sponge and stick and handing it to Julius so he can wipe his bottom.

"I thought of Invicta," says Julius. "It means invincible."

"It'll take more than a scary name to save you," jokes Felix (whose name means lucky).

Fabius flicks back his hair. "I thought maybe Pearl, or Beryl – so the ladies will remember my pretty-boy looks."

Felix tries not to laugh.

"Hurry up," he tells you and Max, as he leaves. "You two can join us for the next lesson."

As you rush into the arena, a training doctor called Titus gives you a sly smile. "Just in time, boys," he says. "I'm about to teach the class how to die and I need a volunteer."

Titus grabs you and pushes you to your knees. "Hold on to my legs," he orders. "You have to be graceful. Now, no whimpering. You're a gladiator. It's your job to show the audience how to die with dignity."

You daren't move.

"The sword strikes like this, with a swift, clean blow." Titus says. "You'll hardly feel a thing."

The tip of the sword tickles your neck and you fall to the floor gracefully. Everyone applauds. You stand and bow.

"That's all for this morning," says Titus.

As the gladiators stream into the dining hall, you and Max head home for lunch.

"The food smells as bad as the latrines," you say.

"More like animal feed," says Julius, who seems to be leaving with you.

"You not eating?" Max asks.

"Not that rubbish," says Julius. "I'm a Roman citizen. That means I'm free to go home to sleep … and to eat a proper lunch."

KEEPING FIT

Until they step into the arena, gladiators are better cared for than most ordinary citizens. Doctors at the school insist on:

• Regular exercise – gladiators must train for several hours each day

• Keeping clean – running water and good drains to take away toilet waste are very important

• A good diet – gladiators are vegetarians! They eat beans, barley, oatmeal and dried fruit – and that's about it. Served in a mush that looks like animal feed, this diet keeps them fit and strong. It also gives them wind! And a handy layer of extra fat to protect them from nasty sword cuts.

When a gladiator gets injured, the doctors can:

• Check his heart is healthy, by reading his pulse.
• Treat sprains and strains with their bare hands.

• Heal deep wounds with the help of some nasty-looking medical tools.
• Mend broken bones by pushing them back into place with a bone lever.

• Help cure stomachache with a special drink made from ashes scraped up from the fireplace and an acid that's used to make soap.

THE POMPA

It's the night before the games and the gladiators are allowed to eat a proper meal for the first time in months! They're invited to a feast at the house of a wealthy Roman. Fans come to watch the warriors eat and decide who to support.

Max's dad has taken you and Max along, too.

Fabius is eating everything in sight, but Sura and Felix aren't hungry.

"I've served three years and won 14 fights," Felix tells you. "And if I win tomorrow, I'll win the wooden sword and freedom for myself and my family. But what will happen to them if I die?"

You had no idea gladiators could be freed! You're pleased for Felix, but disappointed that you'll only get one chance to see him fight.

Sura is worried his first fight could be his last.

"You're the best trainee here," you tell him. "You'll be fighting another new gladiator. No other trainee can beat you! You've got to believe in yourself."

Felix laughs. "You're right!" he says. "Belief in yourself − that's what it's all about! Maybe you should volunteer as a gladiator one day!"

You smile, proudly.

As you and Max head for the school next morning, the streets are packed with people. Some poorer people have queued all night for a token to get in.

Inside, the school is a hive of activity. Armour is being polished, gladiators are trying out a few last-minute moves and the doctors are fussing around their trainees.

Papa is in a very good mood. He proudly shows you the programme. In huge letters it announces:

TIGRIS THE THRACIAN FIGHTS LIKE NO GLADIATOR YOU'VE SEEN BEFORE OR WILL EVER SEE AGAIN

"Tigris is you, isn't it?" you ask Sura.

"Yes, but I hate nicknames," Sura answers, angrily. "There's nothing wrong with the name I've got. That's typical of Papa."

Actually, Papa has been surprisingly nice to you and Max. He's asked you to join the pompa! That's the procession that starts the gladiator contest. He thinks it would look good to have two mini gladiators at the front.

Max's dad has arranged for you to see the morning games, and Felix leads you to a wide passage underneath the school.

"It'll take you to the amphitheatre," he says. "Enjoy yourselves, but make sure you're back by lunchtime."

You climb a steep, brightly painted staircase. Then, at the side of the arena, you gasp. You've never seen so many people before! They are all looking at their tokens and trying to find their seats. Suddenly, there's a huge cheer. The Emperor has arrived! A tiny purple figure waves from his comfy throne.

The morning is full of new experiences. Lions and leopards rush out from trapdoors in the floor. Men, trained at another school, try to hunt them down.

A bear fights a bull, and the crowd laughs as ostriches run from arrows that are fired by skilled archers.

"This is all really exciting," says Max, "but I can't wait for the afternoon sport."

"There are only the executions to go," you say. "Let's give them a miss, grab a sausage from one of the food stalls and get back to the school."

By the time you return, it is really buzzing. You and Max put on striped tunics and purple capes, to show you are part of the games. Then you line up with the rest of the men, ready for the pompa.

At the front of the parade are the musicians, followed by over 400 gladiators, in purple and gold capes, their helmets tucked under their arms. Next come Papa, the referees, armourers and a few magistrates. You and Max lead the gladiators!

Your heart thuds as you march into the arena through two huge wooden doors – the Gates of Life. Musicians play, but the cheers of the crowd drown out their music. The pompa slowly circles the arena and stops in front of the Emperor. Everyone is suddenly quiet. It's time for Papa to draw lots that will sort the gladiators into pairs for each fight.

You listen out for Sura's name. It doesn't come. Finally, with a smile, Papa announces the last fight, the highlight of the afternoon: "Felix, the Murmillo, Champion of the Roman arena, will fight our rising star: Tigris, the Thracian."

THE GAMES

Welcome to the Colosseum! VIPs get tokens for themselves, their families and friends – poor people

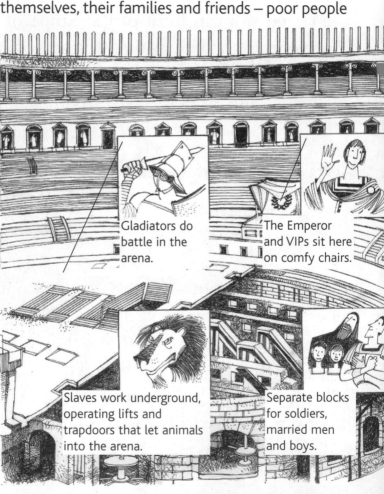

Gladiators do battle in the arena.

The Emperor and VIPs sit here on comfy chairs.

Slaves work underground, operating lifts and trapdoors that let animals into the arena.

Separate blocks for soldiers, married men and boys.

have to pay. Up to 50,000 spectators push past the food stalls to get into the amphitheatre through 76 entrances. Inside, over 1,000 sailors operate sails to keep everyone cool, but it still feels blisteringly hot!

Slaves and poor people sit here on their own cushions.

Rich women and girls sit here, protected from the sun.

Senators and priests sit here on ivory seats.

Two groups of supporters – for gladiators with small and large shields.

THE BIG FIGHT

Felix and Sura can't believe it. New and experienced gladiators are always kept apart. They never dreamed they'd have to fight each other ... to the death.

But the show must go on. Officials check the weapons are fit for action. Gladiators show off their moves. Then, as you leave the arena, the crowd settles down, ready for the afternoon's sport.

The first two gladiators are given weapons, and march in through the Gates of Life. The crowd starts to cheer and shout. But you're so busy worrying about the final fight you hardly notice.

Between fights, slaves spray rosewater into the crowd, but it doesn't hide the horrible stink of blood, sweat and animal poo.

Fabius is on next. You can't bear to watch. But the audience soon roars with laughter. "What's happening?" you ask Max, peering round the Gates of Life.

"Fabius has his opponent on the floor," says Max. "He's dancing around him. He's won!"

Before the final fight, Felix and Sura shake hands. They can't look each other in the eye. But, with helmets on, they aren't Sura and Felix any more. They are Thracian and Murmillo.

They try to stare each other out. Neither man blinks. Each gladiator moves perfectly. The Thracian swings his sword; the Murmillo bars it. The Murmillo strides forward to strike. The Thracian twists away. The crowd oohs and aahs.

Other fights have lasted up to 15 minutes, but this one goes on much longer. The gladiators are a perfect match.

Suddenly, one of the gladiators is on the ground. People yell, scream and stamp their feet. It's Felix! You can't believe it.

Felix drops his sword, raises his right hand, and points his index finger towards the Emperor.

The crowd roars. You look at Max, confused.

"The Emperor will decide whether Felix lives or dies," he says.

You feel sick. The crowd goes wild. "Let him have it!" some shout, stabbing their chests with their thumbs. "Let him live," shout others, waving handkerchiefs madly.

Suddenly, the Emperor is on his feet. The arena is deathly quiet. He raises his fist. It hangs in the air. Your heart thunders in your chest. The thumb plunges downwards.

The arena shakes as everyone jumps to their feet, stamping and shouting.

"What does it mean?" you ask.

"Sura has won the contest!" says Max. "And Felix does not have to die."

You fling your arms around Max. The two of you jump up and down as Sura climbs up to the Emperor's box.

It's been a fantastic afternoon's sport and the Emperor is delighted. He presents Sura with a palm branch for winning his game and puts a laurel crown on his head. The crowd cheers and claps.

"He's impressed," says Max. "Not many winners get the crown."

But that's not all. The Emperor holds up a tray of gold coins.

"One – two – three," the audience chants, as the Emperor drops coins into Sura's hands.

Clutching his victory palm and a bag of gold, Sura runs a lap of honour.

Meanwhile, Felix sits at the side of the arena, with his head in his hands.

Later, Max shakes Felix's hand. "What a fight," he says. But Felix isn't listening. He's still alive, but he hasn't won the freedom he dreamed of.

You try to think of something helpful to say, but before you get a chance, there's a tap on your shoulder. It's your dad. He's with Max's dad. They've been watching the games together. Your dad is looking a bit pale.

"I've been thinking," he says. "Your studies are going well, you're a bright boy. I don't want to waste you on the battlefield. I want you to study for the Senate."

Funnily enough, you quite like the idea. Being a gladiator is a tough job, and it's far too scary for you. On the other hand, as a senator, one day *you* could stage the biggest and best games that Rome has ever seen!

FAMOUS GLADIATORS – THREE OF THE BEST

Successful gladiators were famous in their day, but quickly forgotten after their death. Only a few names are remembered...

Spartacus was famous because:

- He escaped from gladiator school, with 78 other gladiators!
- He encouraged thousands more slaves to join him
- He defeated the Roman army nine times
- He made Roman prisoners fight as gladiators
- He was finally defeated and killed – and 6,000 of his soldiers were crucified!

Emperor Commodus was famous because:

• He was more interested in the games than in ruling the Roman Empire

• He fought in the arena over 1000 times

• He made his opponents fight him with wooden swords

• He dressed up in lion skins to look like the god Hercules

• He was hated by the rich and loved by the poor

• He was murdered in a gladiator school, where he planned to perform the following day.

Flamma was famous because

• He was a brilliant Secutor gladiator

• He won the wooden sword of freedom four times, but chose to carry on fighting

• He fought 34 times and died aged 30

• His friend paid for his burial. His tombstone tells us all we know about his life. Most gladiators left no record after they died. They were buried in unmarked graves.

GLOSSARY

amphitheatre – a round building in which gladiators fight

arena – the space in the middle of an amphitheatre where games take place

armourer – one who makes or looks after arms

citizen – any Roman who is not a slave

Colosseum – a huge amphitheatre in Rome

courtyard – an open space surrounded by walls

crucify – to put someone to death by attaching them to a cross

debts – money owed

draw lots – a way of choosing people through chance, e.g. pulling names out of a hat

empire – a large area made up of many countries ruled by one government

execution – putting a convicted criminal to death

greaves – a piece of armour used to protect the leg from the ankle to the knee

griffin – a mythical creature with the wings and head of an eagle and the body of a lion

lap of honour – victory lap of the arena by the winner of the games